Introduction

The decision to write this smoothie recipe book came from a prolonged enjoyment of the creative art of smoothie making. Smoothies are a fun and simple way to indulge into your favourite foods without the hassle of everyday cooking! I want to share with you 50 delicious smoothie recipes which I have enjoy and regularly make at home.

Why do people enjoy drinking smoothies so much? Upon writing this book I asked myself this question and have concluded that people drink smoothies for many reasons.

Firstly, smoothies are quick and easy to make. Making your own delicious smoothie doesn't take as long as preparing most meals, giving you more time for more important things.

The 5-a-day rule, smoothies are a great way to include the recommended 5 fruit and vegetables a day into your diet, a varied diet is a healthy diet!

Smoothies are yummy! Healthy or not so healthy there are hundreds of combinations to choose from, you're bound to find a smoothie that's just for you!

Lastly, smoothies are fun to make, especially if you have a young family. Smoothie making is a fantastic way to entice kids into the world of healthy eating!

I like my smoothies thick and full of flavour, please feel free to change the quantities of the ingredients to your own personal taste!

Summer Blast

A simple but refreshing smoothie to enjoy on a hot summers day and full of vitamin C! Best served ice cold.

Ingredients:

- **220g Raspberries**
- **125g Strawberries**
- **50g Blueberries**
- **100ml Fresh Milk**
- **4 Ice Cubes**

Method:

1. **Prepare the fruit by removing stalks from the strawberries.**
2. **Place the ingredients into the blender and blitz until desired consistency. (Add more milk for a thinner smoothie)**
3. **Switch off blender once ice cubes have finished blending and let it set for 1 minute. (optional)**
4. **Pour into a glass and enjoy!**

Top tip: Use frozen fruit instead of fresh fruit if you enjoy your smoothies ice cold!

Banana, Banana, Banana

An easy smoothie based on the nation's favourite fruit, every year 5 billion bananas are eaten in Britain alone!

Ingredients:

- **1 Banana**
- **1 Scoop of Vanilla Ice-cream**
- **50ml Fresh Milk**

Method:

1. **Prepare the fruit by removing the skin of the banana.**
2. **Place the ingredients into the blender and blitz until desired consistency. (Add more milk for a thinner smoothie)**
3. **Switch off blender once ice cubes have finished blending and let it set for 1 minute. (optional)**
4. **Pour into a glass and enjoy!**

Top tip: If you enjoy a strong banana taste, add a few drops of banana essence!

The Ultimate Breakfast Smoothie

A firm favourite at home and a popular alternative to beans on toast!

Ingredients:

- 1 Banana
- 2 Tablespoons of Honey
- 4 Tablespoons of Porridge Oats
- 50ml Fresh Milk
- 3 Ice Cubes

Method:

1. Prepare the fruit by removing the skin of banana.
2. Place the ingredients into the blender and blitz until desired consistency. (Add more milk for a thinner smoothie)
3. Switch off blender once ice cubes have finished blending and let it set for 1 minute. (optional)
4. Pour into a glass and enjoy!

Top tip: Not a banana fan? Use 125g fresh strawberries instead!

Simply Berry

This smoothie has a deep purple colour and is full of anti-oxidants which are linked to anti-aging effects!

Ingredients:

- **100g Blueberries**
- **50g Blackberries**
- **100ml Fresh Milk**
- **3 Ice Cubes**

Method:

1. **Wash the fruit and drain well.**
2. **Place the ingredients into the blender and blitz until desired consistency. (Add more milk for a thinner smoothie)**
3. **Switch off blender once ice cubes have finished blending and let it set for 1 minute. (optional)**
4. **Pour into a glass and enjoy!**

Top tip: Late summer is the perfect time to go out and pick your own blackberries!

Tropical Fusion

A healthy slice of the Caribbean... Within a glass!

Ingredients:

- 1 Mango
- 1 Kiwi
- 100g Pineapple Slices (tinned)
- 125ml Coconut Milk
- 3 Ice Cubes

Method:

1. Peel the skin off the mango and kiwi fruit.
2. Drain the pineapple slices.
3. Place the ingredients into the blender and blitz until desired consistency. (Add more coconut milk for a thinner smoothie)
4. Switch off blender once ice cubes have finished blending and let it set for 1 minute. (optional)
5. Pour into a glass and enjoy!

Top tip: Garnish with a mini cocktail umbrella for a cheesy effect!

One for Coffee Lovers

Based on the well-known coffee shop chain's cold coffee beverages, this smoothie is a strong kick start to the day!

Ingredients:

- **2 Teaspoons instant Coffee granules**
- **3 Tablespoons instant Hot Chocolate powder**
- **2 Tablespoons Natural Yoghurt**
- **150ml Fresh Milk**
- **3 Ice Cubes**

Method:

1. **Place the ingredients into the blender and blitz until desired consistency. (Add more coconut milk for a thinner smoothie)**
2. **Switch off blender once ice cubes have finished blending and let it set for 1 minute. (optional)**
3. **Pour into a glass and enjoy!**

Top tip: Perfect with an amaretto biscuit!

The Original Strawberry and Lime

This smoothie is one of my all-time favourites; a strong strawberry flavour with a hint of tangy lime will really excite your taste buds!

Ingredients:

- **200g Strawberries**
- **Juice of 1 Lime**
- **Sprig of Fresh Mint**
- **2 Tablespoons of Natural Yoghurt**
- **2 Ice cubes**

Method:

1. **Prepare the fruit by removing stalks from the strawberries.**
2. **Slice the lime in half and squeeze juice using a juicer.**
3. **Place the ingredients into the blender and blitz until desired consistency. (Add more yoghurt for a thicker smoothie)**
4. **Switch off blender once ice cubes have finished blending and let it set for 1 minute. (optional)**
5. **Pour into a glass and enjoy!**

Top tip: Use frozen strawberries if you prefer your smoothies extra cold!

Orange Fizz

This smoothie is a fantastic one to make with the kids, a healthier alternative to fizzy pop!

Ingredients:

- ½ Mango
- Tin of Mandarins
- 150ml Chilled Fresh Orange Juice
- 50ml Sparkling Water
- 2 Ice Cubes

Method:

1. Prepare the fruit by removing the skin of the mango.
2. Drain the tin of mandarins.
3. Place the ingredients into the blender and blitz.
4. Switch off blender once ice cubes have finished blending and let it set for 1 minute. (optional)
5. Pour into a glass and enjoy!

Top tip: Use the freshest orange juice for best results!

Groovy Green

This smoothie is full of goodness! Containing vitamins A, C and K, you can't go wrong with this daily dose of green!

Ingredients:

- **25g Kale**
- **25g Spinach**
- **1 Avocado**
- **150ml Coconut Milk**
- **2 Ice Cubes**

Method:

1. **Prepare the fruit by removing the skin of the avocado and spooning out the edible flesh.**
2. **Place the ingredients into the blender and blitz.**
3. **Switch off blender once ice cubes have finished blending and let it set for 1 minute. (optional)**
4. **Pour into a glass and enjoy!**

Top tip: If you're not too keen on spinach, try adding carrot instead!

Chocolate Mint Delight

Luxurious, elegant and divine. This smoothie is perfect for a candle-lit romantic night in!

Ingredients:

- **100g Dark Chocolate**
- **Sprig of Mint**
- **3 Scoops of Vanilla Ice-cream**
- **2 Tablespoons of Vanilla Yoghurt**

Method:

1. **Break the chocolate into small chunks.**
2. **Place the ingredients into the blender and blitz.**
3. **Switch off blender once ice cubes have finished blending and let it set for 1 minute. (optional)**
4. **Pour into a glass and enjoy!**

Top tip: Could be used as an alternative to a dessert!

Carrot and Apple Smoothie

A simple recipe using everyday ingredients!

Ingredients:

- 1 Apple
- 2 Carrots
- 25g Spinach
- ½ Cucumber
- 100ml Coconut Water
- 2 Ice Cubes

Method:

1. Prepare the fruit by removing the skin of the apple and carrots and wash the spinach before use.
2. Place the ingredients into the blender and blitz.
3. Switch off blender once ice cubes have finished blending and let it set for 1 minute. (optional)
4. Pour into a glass and enjoy!

Top tip: Add 2 tablespoons of Natural Yoghurt to thicken up this smoothie!

Perfect Peaches

Soft and pungent, this smoothie is light and delicate on the taste buds, a firm favourite in this household!

Ingredients:

- **Tin of Peaches**
- **Sprig of Mint**
- **150ml Coconut Water**
- **2 Ice Cubes**

Method:

1. **Drain the tin of peaches.**
2. **Place the ingredients into the blender and blitz.**
3. **Switch off blender once ice cubes have finished blending and let it set for 1 minute. (optional)**
4. **Pour into a glass and enjoy!**

Top tip: Use 50ml coconut cream instead of coconut milk for added texture.

Banana and Ginger Smoothie

One of my favourites! A perfect smoothie on a cold winter day.

Ingredients:

- 1 Banana
- ½ Teaspoon grated raw Ginger
- 2 Tablespoons of Vanilla Yoghurt
- 1 Tablespoons of Honey
- 2 Ice Cubes

Method:

1. Prepare the fruit by removing the skin of the banana.
2. Use a cheese grater to grate the ginger.
3. Place the ingredients into the blender and blitz.
4. Switch off blender once ice cubes have finished blending and let it set for 1 minute. (optional)
5. Pour into a glass and enjoy!

Top tip: This smoothie is served best ice cold, alongside ginger biscuits for the ideal winter snack.

Coffee and Walnut Smoothie (Warning: Contains Nuts)

This smoothie is inspired by the traditional Coffee and Walnut Cake. Served best ice cold. (with whipped cream)

Ingredients:

- 1 Teaspoon instant Coffee Granules
- 25g Chopped Walnuts
- 2 Scoops of Vanilla Ice-cream
- 2 Teaspoons of Honey
- 50ml Fresh Milk
- 2 Ice Cubes

Method:

1. Chop the walnuts into small pieces.
2. Place the ingredients into the blender and blitz.
3. Switch off blender once ice cubes have finished blending and let it set for 1 minute. (optional)
4. Pour into a glass and enjoy!

Top tip: Add 100ml Vanilla Yoghurt for a thicker smoothie.

Fruit Bowl Smoothie

A healthy concoction of everyday fruits within a scrummy fruit smoothie!

Ingredients:

- **1 Banana**
- **Seeds of 1 Pomegranate**
- **100g Spinach**
- **50ml Coconut Water**
- **150ml Chilled Fresh Orange Juice**
- **2 Ice Cubes**

Method:

1. **Prepare the fruit by removing the skin of the banana and scoop out the seeds of the pomegranate using a spoon.**
2. **Place the ingredients into the blender and blitz.**
3. **Switch off blender once ice cubes have finished blending and let it set for 1 minute. (optional)**
4. **Pour into a glass and enjoy!**

Top tip: Replace coconut water with 50ml sparkling water for extra fizz!

Citrus Squeeze

Short, sharp and with a zing! This lemon smoothie is perfect for citrus lovers!

Ingredients:

- ½ Banana
- 125g Lemon Yoghurt
- Juice of 2 lemons
- 1 Tablespoon of Honey
- 100ml Fresh Milk
- 2 Ice Cubes

Method:

1. Prepare the fruit by removing the skin of the banana.
2. Place the ingredients into the blender and blitz.
3. Switch off blender once ice cubes have finished blending and let it set for 1 minute. (optional)
4. Pour into a glass and enjoy!

Top tip: Use juice from real lemons for a sharper taste.

Banana and Chocolate Smoothie

A famous combination! Another favourite within my household.

Ingredients:

- 1 Banana
- 3 Tablespoons of instant Hot Chocolate powder
- 150ml Fresh Milk
- 2 Ice Cubes

Method:

1. Prepare the fruit by removing the skin of the banana.
2. Place the ingredients into the blender and blitz.
3. Switch off blender once ice cubes have finished blending and let it set for 1 minute. (optional)
4. Pour into a glass and enjoy!

Top tip: Top with chocolate sauce!

Coconut Dream Smoothie

A real coconut experience within a glass! This smoothie has a creamy colour, rough texture and a delicious coconut flavour.

Ingredients:

- 1 Avocado
- 60ml Coconut Cream
- 50ml Fresh Milk
- 3 Tablespoons of Natural Yoghurt
- 2 Ice Cubes

Method:

1. Prepare the fruit by removing the skin of the avocado and spooning out the edible flesh.
2. Place the ingredients into the blender and blitz.
3. Switch off blender once ice cubes have finished blending and let it set for 1 minute. (optional)
4. Pour into a glass and enjoy!

Top tip: If you are not in favour of the rough coconut texture, use 60ml of Coconut Milk instead of Coconut Cream.

Nutty Banana Smoothie (Warning: Contains nuts)

A soft banana smoothie with a hint of walnut on the side. A favourite of the kids!

Ingredients:

- 1 Banana
- 25g Chopped Walnuts
- 100ml Fresh Milk
- 2 Ice Cubes

Method:

1. Prepare the fruit by removing the skin of the banana.
2. Chop the walnuts into small pieces.
3. Place the ingredients into the blender and blitz.
4. Switch off blender once ice cubes have finished blending and let it set for 1 minute. (optional)
5. Pour into a glass and enjoy!

Top tip: Add 100ml Vanilla Yoghurt for a thicker smoothie.

Papaya Perfection

This smoothie is a taste of the tropics! A healthy snack throughout the day.

Ingredients:

- 1 Papaya
- 3 Pineapple slices (tinned)
- 2 Tablespoons Natural Yoghurt
- 50ml Coconut Milk
- 2 Ice Cubes

Method:

1. Remove the skin from the Papaya, and drain the pineapple slices.
2. Place the ingredients into the blender and blitz.
3. Switch off blender once ice cubes have finished blending and let it set for 1 minute. (optional)
4. Pour into a glass and enjoy!

Top tip: Use 50ml coconut cream instead of coconut milk for added texture.

Very Berry

A sweet taste all-round; this smoothie is perfect on a warm summer's day.

Ingredients:

- **100g blueberries**
- **100ml cranberry juice**
- **2 tablespoons honey**
- **3 ice cubes**

Method:

1. **Place the ingredients into the blender and blitz.**
2. **Switch off blender once ice cubes have finished blending and let it set for 1 minute. (optional)**
3. **Pour into a glass and enjoy!**

Top tip: Use apple juice instead of cranberry juice!

Apple and Cinnamon Smoothie

A delicious apple smoothie with a hint of cinnamon.

Ingredients:

- 1 Apple
- ½ Teaspoon Cinnamon
- 40ml Apple juice
- 2 Tablespoons Natural Yoghurt
- 3 Ice cubes

Method:

1. Remove the skin from the apple.
2. Place the ingredients into the blender and blitz.
3. Switch off blender once ice cubes have finished blending and let it set for 1 minute. (optional)
4. Pour into a glass and enjoy!

Top tip: Use 3 scoops of vanilla yoghurt for a thicker smoothie.

Lovely Lime Smoothie

A smoothie with a citrus punch!

Ingredients:

- **Juice of 1 Lime**
- **1 Banana**
- **50ml Coconut Cream**
- **3 Ice cubes**

Method:

1. **Place the ingredients into the blender and blitz.**
2. **Switch off blender once ice cubes have finished blending and let it set for 1 minute. (optional)**
3. **Pour into a glass and enjoy!**

Top tip: Use a hand juicer to prevent lime pips from entering the smoothie.

Fresh Mint and Pineapple Smoothie

A tropical smoothie complimented with a fresh mint tinge.

Ingredients:

- **100g Pineapple slices (tinned)**
- **1 Whole Kiwi**
- **A Sprig of Mint**
- **100ml Coconut milk**
- **3 Ice cubes**

Method:

1. **Place the ingredients into the blender and blitz.**
2. **Switch off blender once ice cubes have finished blending and let it set for 1 minute. (optional)**
3. **Pour into a glass and enjoy!**

Top tip: Use basil instead of mint!

Blood Orange Smoothie

A tropical smoothie complimented with a fresh mint tinge.

Ingredients:

- **Juice of 2 Blood oranges**
- **Tin of Mandarins**
- **50g Frozen peaches**
- **2 Tablespoons Natural Yoghurt**

Method:

1. **Place the ingredients into the blender and blitz.**
2. **Switch off blender and let it set for 1 minute. (optional)**
3. **Pour into a glass and enjoy!**

Top tip: Blood oranges are in season in September in the UK, use "easy peeler" oranges as a replacement.

A Health-Kick Smoothie

This smoothie is a lush green colour and full of antioxidants.

Ingredients:

- **Juice of 1 Lemon**
- **1 Avocado**
- **Handful of Kale**
- **2 Tablespoons Natural Yoghurt**
- **3 Ice cubes**

Method:

1. **Place the ingredients into the blender and blitz.**
2. **Switch off blender once ice cubes have finished blending and let it set for 1 minute. (optional)**
3. **Pour into a glass and enjoy!**

Top tip: Spinach can be used instead of kale in this recipe.

Blueberry and Banana Smoothie (Warning: Contains Nuts)

A darker alternative to strawberries!

Ingredients:

- **100g Blueberries**
- **1 Banana**
- **Handful of Spinach**
- **100ml Almond Milk**
- **3 Ice cubes**

Method:

1. **Place the ingredients into the blender and blitz.**
2. **Switch off blender once ice cubes have finished blending and let it set for 1 minute. (optional)**
3. **Pour into a glass and enjoy!**

Top tip: Use blackberries instead of blueberries in this smoothie. (Blackberries are in season in autumn)

On your way to 5-a-day Smoothie

A smoothie full of goodness, drink this and you'll be on your way to achieving your 5-a-day!

Ingredients:

- 1 Banana
- Juice of 2 Oranges
- 1 Carrot
- 120ml Coconut water
- 2 Ice Cubes

Method:

1. Place the ingredients into the blender and blitz.
2. Switch off blender once ice cubes have finished blending and let it set for 1 minute. (optional)
3. Pour into a glass and enjoy!

Top tip: Coconut milk works just as well in this smoothie recipe!

Blackberry and Ginger Smoothie

Scrummy berry flavour with a hint of ginger!

Ingredients:

- **150g Blackberries**
- **½ Teaspoon Freshly Grated Ginger**
- **3 Tablespoons Vanilla Yoghurt**
- **3 Ice Cubes**

Method:

1. **Place the ingredients into the blender and blitz.**
2. **Switch off blender once ice cubes have finished blending and let it set for 1 minute. (optional)**
3. **Pour into a glass and enjoy!**

Top tip: Strawberries, raspberries and blueberries all work well as an alternative to blackberries!

Itty Bitty Strawberry Smoothie

An original strawberry and banana smoothie garnished with chia seeds.

Ingredients:

- **200g Strawberries**
- **1 Banana**
- **1 Teaspoon Chia Seeds**
- **2 Tablespoons Natural Yoghurt**
- **2 Ice Cubes**

Method:

1. **Place the ingredients into the blender and blitz.**
2. **Switch off blender once ice cubes have finished blending and let it set for 1 minute. (optional)**
3. **Pour into a glass and enjoy!**

Top tip: Either garnish the chia seeds on top of the smoothie, or blitz along with the fruit.

It's a date!

A chocolate and date smoothie, perfect combination!

Ingredients:

- **4 Large Soft Dates**
- **1 Teaspoon Cocoa Powder**
- **1 Avocado**
- **100ml Fresh Milk**
- **2 Ice Cubes**

Method:

1. **Place the ingredients into the blender and blitz.**
2. **Switch off blender once ice cubes have finished blending and let it set for 1 minute. (optional)**
3. **Pour into a glass and enjoy!**

Top tip: For a smooth beverage without the texture, replace the avocado with 2 tablespoons vanilla yoghurt.

Halloween Smoothie

A smoothie for those cold, windy winter nights.

Ingredients:

- 1 Tablespoon Pumpkin Puree
- ½ Teaspoon of Cinnamon
- 1 Avocado
- 100ml Coconut Milk
- 3 Ice cubes

Method:

1. Place the ingredients into the blender and blitz.
2. Switch off blender once ice cubes have finished blending and let it set for 1 minute. (optional)
3. Pour into a glass and enjoy!

Top tip: This recipe works just as well with fresh pumpkin pieces!

Honeydew and Mint Smoothie

Sweet and pungent; a healthy drink.

Ingredients:

- ¼ Honeydew Melon
- A Sprig of Mint
- 2 Tablespoons Natural Yoghurt
- 2 Ice Cubes

Method:

1. Place the ingredients into the blender and blitz.
2. Switch off blender once ice cubes have finished blending and let it set for 1 minute. (optional)
3. Pour into a glass and enjoy!

Top tip: Cantaloupe melons work perfectly well too!

Tropical Chia Smoothie

A tropical smoothie with chia seeds!

Ingredients:

- **100g Pineapple Slices (tinned)**
- **1 Banana**
- **1 Mango**
- **1 Teaspoon Chia Seeds**
- **2 Tablespoons Vanilla Yoghurt**
- **2 Ice Cubes**

Method:

1. **Drain the pineapple slices before blitzing.**
2. **Place the ingredients into the blender and blitz.**
3. **Switch off blender once ice cubes have finished blending and let it set for 1 minute. (optional)**
4. **Pour into a glass and enjoy!**

Top tip: Replace chia seeds with flaxseed as an alternative.

Watermelon Smoothie

A drink that rehydrates your body AND your taste buds!

Ingredients:

- **1/3 Fresh Watermelon**
- **Juice of 1 Lime**
- **A Sprig of Mint**
- **2 Tablespoons Natural Yoghurt**
- **1 Ice Cube**

Method:

1. **Place the ingredients into the blender and blitz.**
2. **Switch off blender once ice cubes have finished blending and let it set for 1 minute. (optional)**
3. **Pour into a glass and enjoy!**

Top tip: Although the pips of watermelon are edible, remove before blitzing for a smoother beverage!

Celery, Mango and Banana Smoothie

A smoothie full of vitamins, texture and taste!

Ingredients:

- **3 Celery Sticks**
- **1 Banana**
- **1 Mango**
- **100ml Coconut Water**
- **2 Ice Cubes**

Method:

1. **Place the ingredients into the blender and blitz.**
2. **Switch off blender once ice cubes have finished blending and let it set for 1 minute. (optional)**
3. **Pour into a glass and enjoy!**

Top tip: Leave this smoothie in the fridge for 15 minutes before drinking.

Pear and Walnut Smoothie (Warning: Contains Nuts)

A classic pear and walnut smoothie recipe. Best served ice cold.

Ingredients:

- **2 Pears**
- **4-5 Whole Walnuts**
- **2 Tablespoons Natural Yoghurt**
- **1 Tablespoon Honey**
- **2 Ice Cubes**

Method:

1. **Place the ingredients into the blender and blitz.**
2. **Switch off blender once ice cubes have finished blending and let it set for 1 minute. (optional)**
3. **Pour into a glass and enjoy!**

Top tip: Soft conference pears work best for this smoothie.

Funky Figs

A smoothie consisting of figs and honey.

Ingredients:

- **3 Figs**
- **2 Tablespoons Honey**
- **3 Scoops Vanilla Ice-cream**
- **50ml Fresh Milk**

Method:

1. **Place the ingredients into the blender and blitz.**
2. **Switch off blender and let it set for 1 minute. (optional)**
3. **Pour into a glass and enjoy!**

Top tip: Figs are in season during late summer and early autumn.

Banana and Chilli Smoothie

The favourite banana smoothie with a kick of fiery hot chilli!

Ingredients:

- **1 Banana**
- **½ Teaspoon Crushed Chilli**
- **100ml Chocolate Milk**
- **3 Ice Cubes**

Method:

1. **Place the ingredients into the blender and blitz.**
2. **Switch off blender once ice cubes have finished blending and let it set for 1 minute. (optional)**
3. **Pour into a glass and enjoy!**

Top tip: Do not rub eyes!

Soft Fruit Smoothie

Apricot and Raspberry smoothie, loved by all!

Ingredients:

- **A Tin of Apricots**
- **120g Raspberries**
- **Juice of 1 Lemon**
- **2 Tablespoons Natural Yoghurt**
- **2 Ice Cubes**

Method:

1. **Place the ingredients into the blender and blitz.**
2. **Switch off blender once ice cubes have finished blending and let it set for 1 minute. (optional)**
3. **Pour into a glass and enjoy!**

Top tip: Replace apricots with a tin of peaches instead.

Salad Smoothie

Beetroot and Spring Onion, in a smoothie!

Ingredients:

- **1 Chopped Beetroot**
- **20g Chopped Spring Onion**
- **100ml Coconut Water**
- **2 Ice Cubes**

Method:

1. **Place the ingredients into the blender and blitz.**
2. **Switch off blender once ice cubes have finished blending and let it set for 1 minute. (optional)**
3. **Pour into a glass and enjoy!**

Top tip: Add a handful of watercress for extra crunch!

Cherry and Chocolate Smoothie

Cherry and chocolate smoothie; indulgent and delicious.

Ingredients:

- **50g Fresh Cherries**
- **3 Teaspoons Cocoa Powder**
- **120ml Fresh Milk**
- **2 Ice Cubes**

Method:

1. **Place the ingredients into the blender and blitz.**
2. **Switch off blender once ice cubes have finished blending and let it set for 1 minute. (optional)**
3. **Pour into a glass and enjoy!**

Top tip: Frozen cherries work just as well; remember not to add the ice cubes.

Elderflower Smoothie

A smoothie with a pungent aroma and moorish taste.

Ingredients:

- **1 Banana**
- **150g Blackberries**
- **100ml Elderflower Juice**
- **50ml Coconut Water**
- **2 Ice Cubes**

Method:

1. **Place the ingredients into the blender and blitz.**
2. **Switch off blender once ice cubes have finished blending and let it set for 1 minute. (optional)**
3. **Pour into a glass and enjoy!**

Top tip: Elderflower cordial can be used instead of elderflower juice.

Tomato and Basil Smoothie

Not a sauce! A famous combination resulting in a yummy smoothie.

Ingredients:

- **3 Tomatoes**
- **A sprig of Basil**
- **3 Tablespoons Natural Yoghurt**
- **2 Ice Cubes**

Method:

1. **Place the ingredients into the blender and blitz.**
2. **Switch off blender once ice cubes have finished blending and let it set for 1 minute. (optional)**
3. **Pour into a glass and enjoy!**

Top tip: Use chopped tomatoes instead of fresh tomatoes.

Vitamin Smoothie

A healthy smoothie full of essential vitamins.

Ingredients:

- **1 Avocado**
- **Handful of Spinach**
- **Handful of Watercress**
- **100ml Coconut Water**
- **2 Ice Cubes**

Method:

1. **Place the ingredients into the blender and blitz.**
2. **Switch off blender once ice cubes have finished blending and let it set for 1 minute. (optional)**
3. **Pour into a glass and enjoy!**

Top tip: Swap spinach for kale to enjoy extra iron!

Fruit and Nut Smoothie (Warning: Contains Nuts)

A fruit and nut smoothie using banana, strawberries and almonds. Best served ice cold.

Ingredients:

- **1 Banana**
- **150g Strawberries**
- **50g Whole Almonds**
- **100ml Almond Milk**
- **2 Ice Cubes**

Method:

1. **Place the ingredients into the blender and blitz.**
2. **Switch off blender once ice cubes have finished blending and let it set for 1 minute. (optional)**
3. **Pour into a glass and enjoy!**

Top tip: Hazelnuts work perfectly in this recipe too!

Marvellous Mango Smoothie

A simple mango smoothie, best served ice cold!

Ingredients:

- 1 Mango
- Tin of Mandarins
- 3 Tablespoons Natural Yoghurt
- 2 Ice Cubes

Method:

1. Place the ingredients into the blender and blitz.
2. Switch off blender once ice cubes have finished blending and let it set for 1 minute. (optional)
3. Pour into a glass and enjoy!

Top tip: Leave to set in the fridge for 15 minutes before serving.

Pineapple and Blueberry Smoothie

A sweet smoothie combining pineapple, blueberry and orange!

Ingredients:

- **100g Pineapple Slices (tinned)**
- **2 Small Oranges**
- **50g Blueberries**
- **100ml Coconut Water**
- **2 Ice Cubes**

Method:

1. **Place the ingredients into the blender and blitz.**
2. **Switch off blender once ice cubes have finished blending and let it set for 1 minute. (optional)**
3. **Pour into a glass and enjoy!**

Top tip: Mandarins work well instead of oranges!

Pistachio and Ginger Smoothie

Contemporary and scrummy!

Ingredients:

- **25g Salted Pistachio Nuts**
- **½ Teaspoon Freshly Grated Ginger**
- **3 Tablespoons Natural Yoghurt**
- **50ml Fresh Milk**
- **2 Ice Cubes**

Method:

1. **Remove shells of pistachio nuts before blitzing.**
2. **Place the ingredients into the blender and blitz.**
3. **Switch off blender once ice cubes have finished blending and let it set for 1 minute. (optional)**
4. **Pour into a glass and enjoy!**

Top tip: Served best with an amaretto biscuit.

Thank you for reading my Smoothie Recipe book and I hope you enjoyed my 50 Delicious Smoothie Recipes,

Connor

Disclaimer: I am not a registered dietitian or a nutritional expert. I enjoy creating delicious smoothies and the reader should consult a healthcare professional before making any changes to their diet.

13981858R00031

Printed in Great Britain
by Amazon.co.uk, Ltd.,
Marston Gate.